HOCKEY HALL OF FAME

GREAT GOALIES

GREAT GOALIES

ERIC ZWEIG

ILLUSTRATIONS BY GEORGE TODOROVIC

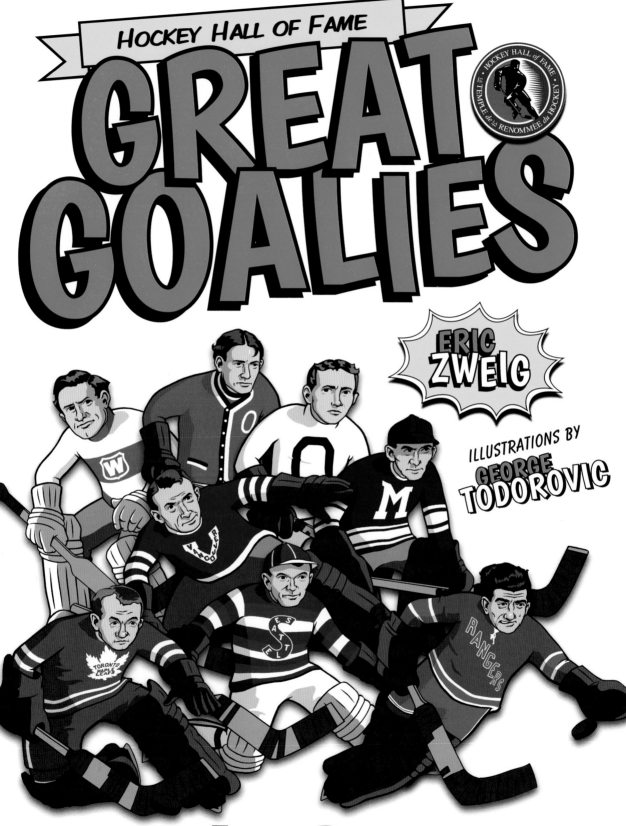

FIREFLY BOOKS

A Firefly Book

Published by Firefly Books Ltd. 2014

Second printing

Publisher Cataloging-in-Publication Data (U.S.)
A CIP record for this title is available from the Library of Congress

Library and Archives Canada Cataloguing in Publication
A CIP record for this title is available from Library and Archives Canada

Published in the United States by
Firefly Books (U.S.) Inc.
P.O. Box 1338, Ellicott Station
Buffalo, New York 14205

Published in Canada by
Firefly Books Ltd.
50 Staples Avenue, Unit 1
Richmond Hill, Ontario L4B 0A7

Cover and interior design: Kimberley Young
Illustrations: George Todorovic
Creative Direction: Steve Cameron

Printed in China

The publisher gratefully acknowledges the financial support for our publishing program
by the Government of Canada through the Canada Book Fund as administered by
the Department of Canadian Heritage.

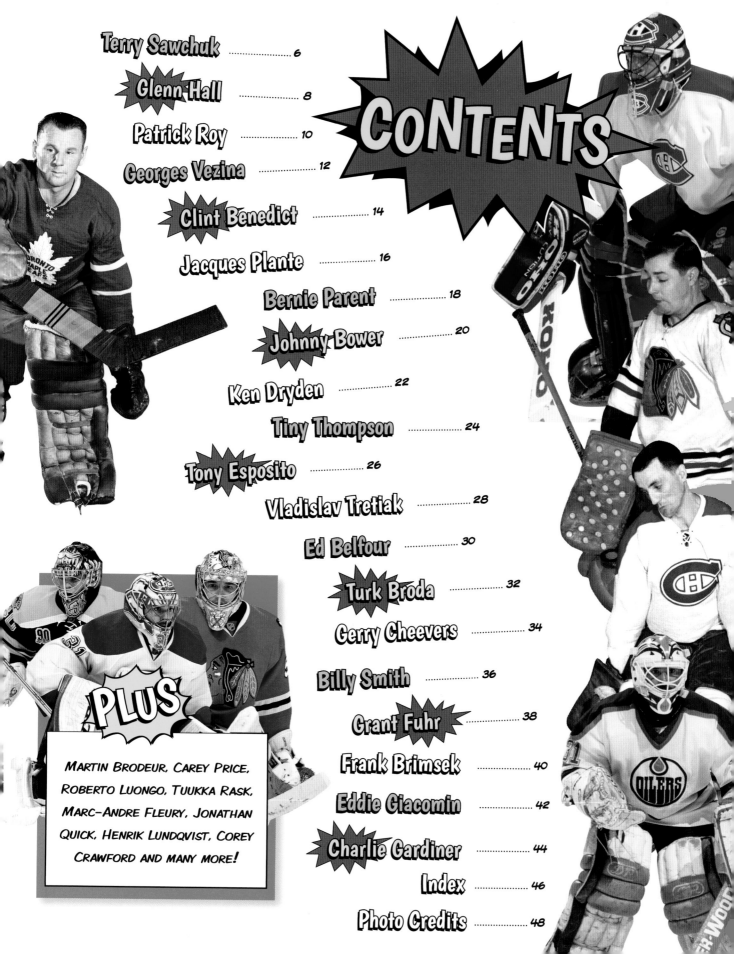

CONTENTS

PLUS

MARTIN BRODEUR, CAREY PRICE, ROBERTO LUONGO, TUUKKA RASK, MARC-ANDRE FLEURY, JONATHAN QUICK, HENRIK LUNDQVIST, COREY CRAWFORD AND MANY MORE!

TERRY SAWCHUK

HOCKEY HALL OF FAME: 1971

FOR A VERY LONG TIME, IT SEEMED NO NHL GOALIE WOULD WIN MORE GAMES OR EARN MORE SHUTOUTS THAN TERRY SAWCHUK. EVEN TODAY, MORE THAN 40 YEARS AFTER HE DIED, ONLY FOUR GOALIES HAVE PASSED SAWCHUK'S 447 CAREER WINS, AND JUST ONE — MARTIN BRODEUR — HAS ||||➡

FROM THE VAULT

BROWN LEATHER BEAUTIES

Terry Sawchuk wore this pair of Kenesky pads from 1957 to 1964. Emil "Pop" Kenesky was a leather worker who made horse harnesses before he started making goalie pads. When he started, goalie pads were the slim style of leg pad common among cricket players. Kenesky's original attempts were beefed up versions of these. Over the years the reputation of his pads grew and they became the pads NHL goalies wanted. Kenesky stuffed his leather pads with deer hair and kapok (a silky fiber made from the seeds of tropical plants). They remained popular until the early 1990s, when modern materials meant pads could be made stronger and lighter.

broken his record of 103 shutouts.

Sawchuk was a tense competitor and a person who found it hard to relax. Some of that was due to the nerves created by the scary task of stopping pucks without a mask. Some of it came from a hard childhood; two of Sawchuk's older brothers had died when he was a boy. When he was 10, he was given the goalie pads of his late brother Mike. By the time he was 16, he'd signed with the Detroit Red Wings. He became Detroit's starter in 1950–51 when he was 21.

Until then, goalies usually played a standup style, trying to keep their unmasked faces far away from the puck. But Sawchuk played differently, getting low to the ice in a deep crouch. It was dangerous, but he could see the puck better that way. In his first full NHL season, Sawchuk set a league record with 44 wins. He also led the league with 11 shutouts and was named rookie of the year. The next season, 1951–52, he posted 44 wins, 12 shutouts and led Detroit to the Stanley Cup! The Red Wings won the Cup again in 1954 and 1955, but Sawchuk was traded to Boston shortly after.

He was never happy in Boston and retired during the 1956–57 season. Boston traded him back to Detroit, where he spent seven more seasons before being moved to Toronto. In 1967, Sawchuk helped the Maple Leafs win the Stanley Cup.

Did You Know?

TERRY SAWCHUK WON THE VEZINA TROPHY THREE TIMES WITH DETROIT AND SHARED IT WITH JOHNNY BOWER IN TORONTO IN 1964–65.

MODERN MATCH
MARTIN BRODEUR

MARTIN BRODEUR MADE a brief debut with the New Jersey Devils in 1991–92 and became the team's top goalie two years later. He's gone on to become the NHL's all-time leading goalie in games played, wins and shutouts and has won the Stanley Cup three times. He also set a single-season record with 48 wins in 2007–08. In addition, Brodeur is great at handling the puck, and has scored three goals in his career! In an era where most goalies play low to the ice, Brodeur prefers to stand up more often and rely on his reflexes.

GLENN HALL

HOCKEY HALL OF FAME: 1975

GLENN HALL WAS SO GOOD, PEOPLE SIMPLY CALLED HIM "MR. GOALIE." DURING HIS 16 FULL NHL SEASONS, HALL EARNED SEVEN SELECTIONS TO THE LEAGUE'S FIRST ALL-STAR TEAM AND FOUR PICKS AS A SECOND-TEAM ALL-STAR. NO OTHER GOALIE IN NHL HISTORY HAS EVER HAD MORE THAN SIX ▶

HARRY LUMLEY Blast FROM THE Past

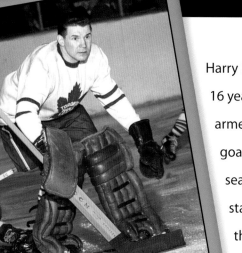

HOCKEY HALL OF FAME: 1980

Harry Lumley signed his first pro contract when he was only 16 years old. With player shortages caused by men serving in the armed forces during Word War II, Lumley became the youngest goalie in NHL history in 1943–44. He played three games that season at the age of 17! A year later, Lumley was in the NHL to stay. He won the Stanley Cup with Detroit in 1949–50 and won the Vezina Trophy with Toronto in 1953–54. When he retired from the league in 1960, Lumley's 330 wins were the most in NHL history.

selections to the First Team, or eight All-Star honors overall!

As a rising star, Hall was part of the Detroit Red Wings organization where he learned from other star goalies Harry Lumley and Terry Sawchuk. Hall admired the way Sawchuk played in a low crouch when most other goalies used the stand-up style. But Hall took the move even further. He would spread his feet wide and drop to his knees while keeping his body upright. By doing so, he pioneered the "butterfly" style that Patrick Roy later refined. The move is still popular today! Hall was also known for a peculiar way of getting ready to play. He would get himself so worked up that he became sick to his stomach before almost every game! "I simply felt I played better when I got sick before a game," he said. "I hope it never bothered my teammates."

Did You Know?

GLENN HALL HELPED ST. LOUIS REACH THE STANLEY CUP FINAL DURING EACH OF THE BLUES' FIRST THREE SEASONS IN THE NHL.

When Hall debuted in the NHL he impressed the Red Wings so much that Detroit traded Sawchuk to make room for him in 1955–56. He led the league with 12 shutouts that season and was named rookie of the year, but Detroit traded him to Chicago in 1957. The Black Hawks were the worst team in the NHL, but soon Hall helped make them great. Chicago won the Stanley Cup in 1960–61 and Hall won the Vezina Trophy for the first of three times in 1962–63. Hall spent his last four seasons with the St. Louis Blues.

THE REAL IRON MAN:
Glenn Hall's Streak

Glenn Hall holds one of the most amazing records in hockey history. Beginning at the start of the 1955–56 season and lasting until early in 1962–63, he played every single minute of every single game in goal for Detroit and Chicago for more than seven straight seasons! The streak stretched for 502 games, and reaches 552 games when the playoffs are counted. Making it all the more amazing, Hall played all those games without wearing a mask! The streak finally ended on November 7, 1962, when a back injury forced Hall out of action during the first period.

PATRICK ROY

HOCKEY HALL OF FAME: 2006

KNOWN AS "ST. PATRICK" TO FANS IN
MONTREAL, PATRICK ROY LED THE CANADIENS
TO A SURPRISING STANLEY CUP VICTORY IN HIS
ROOKIE SEASON OF 1985–86. ROY WAS SO GOOD
DURING MONTREAL'S CHAMPIONSHIP RUN THAT HE
EARNED THE CONN SMYTHE TROPHY ‖‖▶

FROM THE VAULT

TALE OF THE TWINE

This is the mesh from the net that Patrick Roy protected in the
first and third periods of Colorado's 4–3 win over Washington
on October 17, 2000. The victory gave Roy 448 regular-season
wins in his career, breaking the NHL record of 447 wins that
Terry Sawchuk had held for 30 years. Roy went on to post
551 regular-season wins in his career. That was a record when
he retired in 2003, but has since been beaten by Martin Brodeur.
Roy was also the first goalie in NHL history to play 1,000 games
in the regular season.

as playoff MVP. At age 20, he was the youngest player ever to win the award. He would win it again with Montreal in 1993 and with the Colorado Avalanche in 2001, making him the only person in NHL history to be playoff MVP three times!

Roy had a lot of strange habits that fans found interesting. He would always hop over the blue lines when he skated across the ice, and he admitted to talking to his goal posts! In the net Roy seemed to be a bundle of nerves as he constantly bobbed his head up and down and craned his neck from side to side. What he was really doing was getting mentally ready by visualizing himself playing perfectly. Roy may have looked odd some times, but he was a true student of the game. He came to the NHL at a time when improvements in goalie equipment made it lighter and stronger. That helped Roy and his goalie coach Francois Allaire perfect the "butterfly" style that allowed Roy to spread out low across the bottom of the net. His style influenced goalies all across his home province of Quebec and was soon copied by people all around the world.

Roy spent 18 full seasons in the NHL with Montreal and Colorado. He won the Vezina Trophy three times and was the winner of the Jennings Trophy five times. He won the Stanley Cup twice with the Canadiens and twice with the Avalanche and is the NHL's all-time playoff leader with 151 wins!

Did You Know?

PATRICK ROY SET AN NHL RECORD WITH 10 OVERTIME WINS IN THE 1993 PLAYOFFS TO LEAD MONTREAL TO THE STANLEY CUP.

Blast FROM THE Past

HAP HOLMES (HHOF: 1972)

Like Patrick Roy, Harry "Hap" Holmes was a great goalie who got even better in the playoffs. Holmes played in all the best leagues of his era during a career that stretched from 1912 to 1928. He broke in with the Toronto Blue Shirts of the National Hockey Association in 1912–13 and helped them win the Stanley Cup the next season. Holmes later won the Stanley Cup with the Seattle Metropolitans of the Pacific Coast Hockey Association in 1917, the Toronto Arenas of the NHL in 1918, and the Victoria Cougars of the Western Canada Hockey League in 1925.

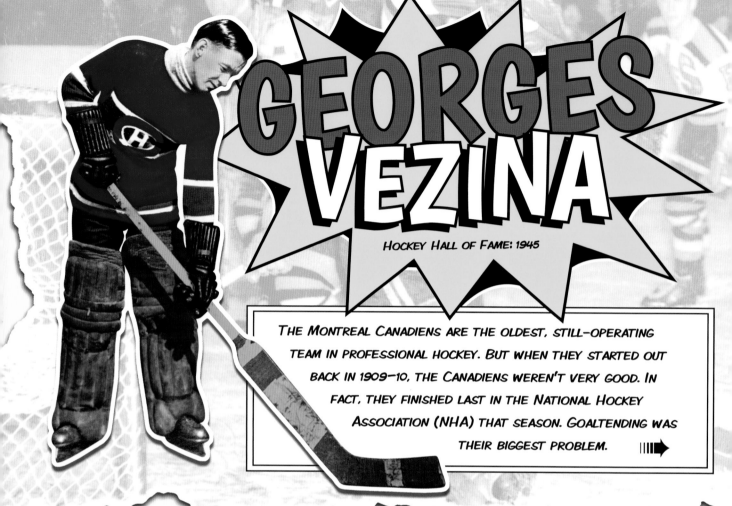

GEORGES VEZINA

HOCKEY HALL OF FAME: 1945

THE MONTREAL CANADIENS ARE THE OLDEST, STILL-OPERATING TEAM IN PROFESSIONAL HOCKEY. BUT WHEN THEY STARTED OUT BACK IN 1909–10, THE CANADIENS WEREN'T VERY GOOD. IN FACT, THEY FINISHED LAST IN THE NATIONAL HOCKEY ASSOCIATION (NHA) THAT SEASON. GOALTENDING WAS THEIR BIGGEST PROBLEM. ▐▐▐➡

VEZINA TROPHY: 1994, 1995, 1997–1999, 2001
JENNINGS TROPHY: 1994, 2001, 2008

Dominik HASEK

GOALIE TROPHIES

The Montreal Canadiens donated the Vezina Trophy to the NHL in 1926–27 in honor of Georges Vezina. For years, it was given to the goalie (or goalies) on the team that allowed the fewest goals each season. Since 1981–82, the Vezina has gone to the goalie that's voted to be the best in the league by the general managers of every NHL team. In 1981–82, a new trophy was donated to reward the goalies on the team allowing the fewest goals. The Jennings Trophy is named after William M. Jennings, a long-time executive with the New York Rangers.

The NHA season was just 12 games long, but the Canadiens tried four different goalies and the team won just two games. During that same season, Georges Vezina led his hometown Chicoutimi Hockey Club to a victory over the Canadiens in an exhibition game. After that, Montreal signed him for the 1910–11 season. Vezina went on to play every single game for the Canadiens for the next 15 years! He helped them win the Stanley Cup for the first time in 1915–16 and led the league in wins and goals-against average when the NHL began in 1917–18.

Vezina played a standup style and almost never dropped to the ice, even when the rules were changed to allow goalies to do so. He was always calm and cool under pressure, which led to his nickname, the "Chicoutimi Cucumber" (from the old expression "cool

Did You Know?

GEORGES VEZINA POSTED THE FIRST SHUTOUT IN NHL HISTORY WITH A 9–0 VICTORY OVER TORONTO ON FEBRUARY 18, 1918.

as a cucumber"). Vezina led the NHL in goals-against average again in 1923–24 and helped the Canadiens win another Stanley Cup that year. In 1924–25, he posted a career-best 1.81 goals-against average to lead the NHL one more time, but when the next season started, it was clear that something was wrong. Vezina looked weak in training camp and in the first game of the 1925–26 season, he was pulled after the first period. It turned out he was suffering from tuberculosis, a very serious lung disease. Vezina never played another game, and he passed away on March 27, 1926.

Parallel Puckstopper

PADDY MORAN (HHOF: 1958)

Paddy Moran played his entire career during an era when hockey rules said a goalie had to remain standing at all times. As a result, his stats don't look very impressive to fans of today. Moran spent 12 seasons from 1905 to 1917 playing in the top hockey leagues of his day. He played 11 of those years with the Quebec Bulldogs and helped them win the Stanley Cup in 1912 and 1913. Unlike Georges Vezina, Moran was known for having a temper, and he would sometimes slash skaters who got too close to his net.

CLINT BENEDICT

Hockey Hall of Fame: 1965

CLINT BENEDICT DOESN'T HAVE A TROPHY NAMED IN HIS HONOR LIKE OLD-TIME MONTREAL GOALIE GEORGES VEZINA, BUT BENEDICT WAS PROBABLY THE BETTER GOALIE. OVER THE YEARS THAT THEY PLAYED IN THE LEAGUE TOGETHER, BENEDICT'S STATS WERE ALMOST ALWAYS BETTER. DURING THE FIRST 10 YEARS AFTER THE NHL WAS FORMED IN 1917–18, ▐▐▐▶

PERCY LESUEUR (HHOF: 1961) — Blast FROM THE Past

Percy LeSueur was the goalie Clint Benedict replaced in Ottawa. LeSueur joined the team late in the 1905–06 season. He couldn't help Ottawa hold on to the Stanley Cup that year, but he helped them win it again in 1909 and 1911. Decades before goalies wore blockers and catchers, LeSueur invented special goalie gloves that had very long cuffs. They were called "gauntlet gloves," and they gave goalies better protection. They were very popular in his era. He also designed a more modern style of goalie net that was used from 1912 to 1925.

Vezina had the league's best goals-against average three times, but Benedict led the league six times! He also led the league in wins six times during the first seven seasons and led (or shared the lead) in shutouts for seven straight seasons. No one else in history has led the NHL in shutouts more often!

Most importantly, Benedict was responsible for one of the biggest rule changes in NHL history. When the league started, goalies had to stay on their feet at all times. Benedict, though, always found a way to go down to stop the puck. When asked he'd say he was tripped, or that he "accidentally" fell. Midway through the very first NHL season, the league decided it was okay for goalies to drop to the ice. After that, Benedict spent so much time on his knees that people called him "Praying Benny."

Benedict joined the Ottawa Senators of the National Hockey Association (NHA) for the 1912–13 season when he was 20 years old. He took over as Ottawa's number-one goalie in 1914–15 and helped the Senators win the NHA championship. Benedict stayed with Ottawa when the NHA was re-formed into the NHL and helped the team win the Stanley Cup in 1920, 1921 and 1923! Before the 1924–25 season, the Senators sold Benedict to a new NHL team called the Montreal Maroons. In just their second season of 1925–26, Benedict helped them win the Stanley Cup.

Did You Know?

CLINT BENEDICT WAS THE FIRST NHL GOALIE TO WEAR A MASK. HE WORE A LEATHER MASK FOR A FEW GAMES DURING HIS FINAL SEASON OF 1929–30.

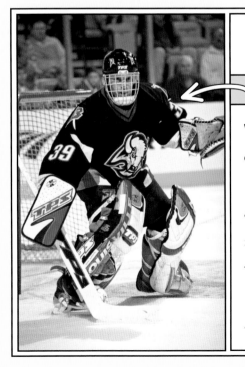

Parallel Puckstopper

DOMINIK HASEK

While Clint Benedict was "accidentally" falling down in the 1910s, he couldn't possibly have imagined the style of Dominik Hasek in the 1990s. Twisting, turning, flipping and flopping, Hasek seemed to have a slinky for a spine! He would do anything to stop the puck. In nine seasons with the Buffalo Sabres, Hasek won the Vezina Trophy six times! He also won the Hart Trophy as NHL MVP in 1996–97 and 1997–98, making him the only goalie in NHL history to win the MVP award twice! He won the Stanley Cup with Detroit in 2002 and 2008.

JACQUES PLANTE

HOCKEY HALL OF FAME: 1978

JACQUES PLANTE WAS THE OLDEST OF 11 CHILDREN GROWING UP IN SHAWINIGAN, QUEBEC. THE FAMILY HAD SO LITTLE EXTRA MONEY THAT WHEN HE STARTED PLAYING HOCKEY THEY COULDN'T AFFORD TO BUY HIM A HOCKEY STICK. INSTEAD, PLANTE PLAYED WITH A STICK HIS FATHER CLEVERLY CARVED FROM A TREE ROOT! PLANTE LOVED HOCKEY AND HE BECAME ▐▐▐▶

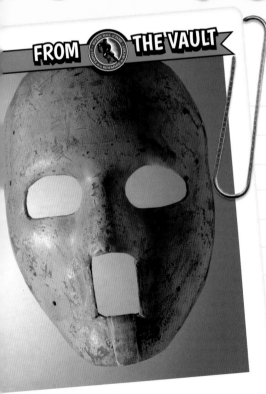

FROM THE VAULT

THE CHANGING FACE OF HOCKEY

Jacques Plante was the first goalie to regularly wear a mask. Aside from a few early experiments, goalies had always played bare-faced. People thought if a goalie wore a mask, he was showing the opposing team he was scared. Plante had been practicing with a mask since 1955, but his coach wouldn't let him wear it in games. Then, on November 1, 1959, Plante's nose was badly cut by a shot from Andy Bathgate of the New York Rangers. When Plante was stitched up and returned to action, he was wearing this mask. He vowed never to play again if he couldn't wear it regularly!

a real rink rat, hanging out at local arenas and getting into as many games as possible. By the time he was 20, Plante had signed with the Montreal Canadiens. The Canadiens had several goalies on the team ahead of him, but Plante was spectacular in a few brief appearances in the NHL. In 1954–55, the Canadiens made him their number-one goalie.

Plante always studied the game trying to find ways he could play better. He was one of the first goalies to roam from his crease, stopping dump-ins behind his net or racing out to play the puck to his defensemen. Sometimes, his daredevil ways made his coaches nervous, but it was obvious that Plante knew what he was doing. From 1955–56 to 1959–60, he helped the Canadiens win the Stanley Cup five years in a row and was also named the Vezina Trophy winner as the league's top

goaltender! He won the Vezina again in 1961–62 and also won the Hart Trophy that year as the NHL's MVP. It took 35 years before another goalie was named MVP.

Plante was traded to New York in 1963 and retired in 1965. After three seasons away from the game, he made a comeback with St. Louis in 1968–69. Plante won the Vezina Trophy for a record seventh time that year, sharing the award with teammate Glenn Hall. Plante continued to play until 1975, retiring for good when he was 46 years old!

Blast FROM THE Past

CHUCK RAYNER (HHOF: 1973)

Chuck Rayner spent most of his NHL career on bad teams in New York. In fact, he played 10 years in the NHL and only made the playoffs twice! Still, in 1949–50, Rayner led the Rangers to the seventh game of the Stanley Cup finals. They didn't win, but Rayner was rewarded for his excellent season by winning the Hart Trophy as league MVP. Like Jacques Plante, Rayner was an excellent skater who loved to handle the puck. While playing with a Canadian Navy team during World War II, Rayner skated the length of the ice and scored a goal!

BERNIE PARENT

Hockey Hall of Fame: 1984

Bernie Parent grew up in Montreal in the 1950s and loved playing road hockey with his friends. Parent cheered for the Montreal Canadiens and imagined himself making saves just like Montreal's goalie Jacques Plante. For Parent, the transition from road hockey to ice hockey was difficult. ||||➡

THE SUCCESSOR

When he was just 20 years old, Pelle Lindbergh led Sweden to a bronze medal in hockey at the 1980 Winter Olympics. Still, his dream was to become the NHL's first great European goalie. Lindbergh's hero growing up was Bernie Parent, so he was very excited to be drafted by Philadelphia. Working with his idol as his goalie coach, Lindbergh became the Flyers' number-one goalie in 1982–83 and won the Vezina Trophy two years later. He was well on his way to realizing his dream when he died in a car accident early in the 1985–86 season.

PHILADELPHIA FLYERS: 1981–82 TO 1985–86

Pelle
LINDBERGH

but he practiced hard. Success was slow to come at first, but as he gained more experience he got better. By the time he was a teenager he was an NHL prospect! When Parent was 18 in 1963, he signed with the Boston Bruins. He played occasionally in Boston, and when the league added six new teams for the start of the 1967–68 season, the Philadelphia Flyers chose Parent to be their goalie.

After three and a half years in Philadelphia, Parent was traded to Toronto in 1971. The other Toronto goalie was Parent's hero, Jacques Plante. He was very excited. "I learned more from [Plante] in two years with the Leafs than I did in all my other hockey days," Parent said. He returned to the Flyers for the 1973–74 season, and very quickly proved he was the best goalie in the NHL. He led the league with 47 wins, 12 shutouts, and a 1.89 goals-against average that season. He was nearly as good in 1974–75, leading the league with 44 wins, 12 shutouts and a 2.03 average!

The Flyers played rough and took a lot of penalties, but Parent almost always made the saves they needed. Not only did he win the Vezina Trophy in 1973–74 and 1974–75, he led the Flyers to back-to-back Stanley Cups and won the Conn Smythe Trophy as playoff MVP both years! Parent was forced to retire after being hit in the eye with a stick in 1979.

Did You Know?

BERNIE PARENT POSTED SHUTOUTS IN THE DECIDING GAME OF THE STANLEY CUP FINAL WHEN PHILADELPHIA WON IT IN 1974 AND IN 1975.

PLAYOFF PAYOFF:
Goalies and the Conn Smythe Trophy

The Conn Smythe Trophy was first given to the MVP of the playoffs in 1965. Since then, more goalies have won the award than players at any other position. Bernie Parent was the first person to win it in back-to-back seasons, and goalie Patrick Roy is the only player to win it more than twice. Sometimes, the Conn Smythe is awarded to a player on the losing team. Five players have won the award on the losing side, and four of them are goalies: Roger Crozier (Detroit 1966), Glenn Hall (St. Louis 1968), Ron Hextall (Philadelphia 1987) and Jean-Sebastien Giguere (Anaheim 2003).

Jonathan Quick, 2012 Conn Smythe winner

JOHNNY BOWER

Hockey Hall of Fame: 1976

IT HAS NEVER BEEN EASY TO MAKE IT TO THE NHL. AND IT WAS EXTRA HARD DURING THE ORIGINAL SIX ERA, WHEN FOR 25 SEASONS, FROM 1942–43 TO 1966–67, THE NHL HAD ONLY SIX TEAMS. FOR MOST OF THAT TIME TEAMS ONLY HAD ONE GOALIE ON THEIR ROSTER, WHICH MEANT THAT OF ALL THE GOALIES ▐▐▐▶

Parallel Puckstopper

GUMP WORSLEY (HHOF: 1980)

When Johnny Bower first played in the NHL with the New York Rangers in 1953–54, it was Gump Worsley he replaced. Worsley won his job back a year later, but New York was a bad team. Things got a lot better for Worsley when he was traded to Montreal in 1963–64. He won the Vezina Trophy twice and the Stanley Cup four times with the Canadiens. Worsley, whose real first name was Lorne, played his final seasons with the Minnesota North Stars. He refused to wear a mask until his last NHL season of 1973–74.

in the world only six were playing in the NHL. An awful lot of good goalies had to wait a long time for their chance at the NHL, and that only happened when another goalie retired, got injured or started playing poorly. For Johnny Bower, he waited patiently for twelve years before finally becoming a full-time NHLer.

Records today list Bower's birthday as November 8, 1924, but when he was playing nobody was really sure how old he was. When he was only 15, Bower lied about his age to join the Canadian Army during World War II. After that, he was shy to let anyone know his true age. He continued playing hockey after his time in the army and spent eight seasons with the Cleveland Barons in the American Hockey League (AHL) before finally getting a chance in the NHL. He played for the New York Rangers in 1953–54, but was back in the minors the next year. Bower was named the AHL's best goalie and most valuable player three times each. He figured he'd spend the rest of his career in the minors, but was convinced to try his luck with the Toronto Maple Leafs in 1958–59 when he was 34 years old! His hard work had finally landed him a full-time job in the NHL. Over the next 11 seasons, Bower won the Vezina Trophy twice and helped Toronto win the Stanley Cup four times!

Did You Know?

JOHNNY BOWER WAS 45 YEARS OLD WHEN HE PLAYED HIS FINAL GAME FOR THE TORONTO MAPLE LEAFS IN 1969–70.

Blast FROM THE Past

HUGH LEHMAN (HHOF: 1958)

Hugh Lehman's pro career stretched from 1906–07 until 1927–28 when he was 42 years old! He spent his last two seasons with the Chicago Black Hawks, but Lehman played most of his career in leagues that either pre-dated the NHL or were rivals to it. Lehman spent 13 seasons in the Pacific Coast Hockey Association from 1911–12 to 1923–24. He had the league's best goals-against average five times and was a 10-time All-Star. Lehman played for the Stanley Cup eight times in his career, but only won it once, with the Vancouver Millionaires in 1914–15.

KEN DRYDEN

Hockey Hall of Fame: 1983

At 6-foot-4 (193 cm) and 205 pounds (93 kg), Ken Dryden wasn't just a big goalie, he was bigger than many players! Dryden was called up to the Montreal Canadiens late in the 1970–71 season and was a surprise starter when they faced Boston in the playoffs. The Bruins had enjoyed a record-shattering ▐▐▐▶

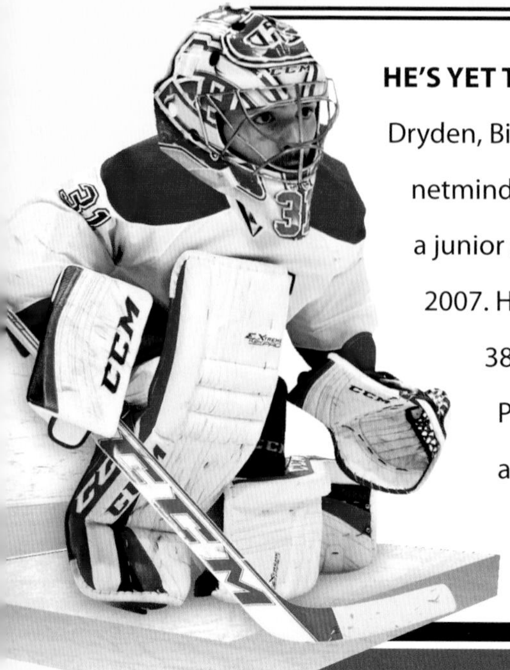

HE'S YET TO enjoy the success of great Canadiens goalies such as Ken Dryden, Bill Durnan, Jacques Plante or Georges Vezina, but as the number-one netminder in Montreal, Carey Price is part of a legendary legacy. Price was a junior star who led Canada to gold at the World Junior Championships in 2007. He joined the Canadiens in 2007–08 and led the NHL with 38 wins in 2010–11. After struggling for a few seasons, Price backstopped Canada to a gold medal at the 2014 Sochi Olympics. His next big step will be trying to win a Stanley Cup in Montreal.

MODERN MATCH

CAREY PRICE

offensive season, and with the likes of Bobby Orr and Phil Esposito, Boston was expected to easily beat Montreal. But Dryden, who had only played in six NHL games, led the Canadiens to a stunning upset. When Montreal went on to win the Stanley Cup, Dryden was named the MVP of the playoffs!

The Canadiens had waited a long time for Dryden to make it to the NHL. It was rare for NHL hopefuls to attend university in those days, but Dryden spent four years at Cornell University in Ithaca, New York. He also played one year for Canada's national hockey team before finally joining the Canadiens. After his heroic playoff, Dryden officially became Montreal's number-one goalie in 1971–72, and because he played in so few games the previous year, he was still considered a rookie for that season. He went on to be named NHL rookie of the year!

In 1972–73, Dryden won the Vezina Trophy for the first time and Montreal won the Stanley Cup again.

While he was playing for the Canadiens, Dryden was also attending school to become a lawyer and sat out the entire 1973–74 season to finish his studies. When he returned to the Canadiens in 1974–75, the team was about to become one of the greatest in hockey history. Montreal won the Stanley Cup four years in a row from 1976 to 1979 and Dryden won the Vezina Trophy every year!

Blast FROM THE Past   BILL DURNAN

Ken Dryden only played eight seasons in the NHL, but he won the Vezina Trophy five times and the Stanley Cup six times. Bill Durnan's career in Montreal 25 years earlier was amazingly similar. Durnan starred with the Canadiens for seven seasons from 1943 to 1950. Montreal won the Stanley Cup twice during those years and Durnan won the Vezina Trophy six times! Durnan was ambidextrous, which means he could use his left or right hand equally well. He had special goalie gloves designed that allowed him to hold his stick or catch the puck with either hand.

HOCKEY HALL OF FAME: 1964

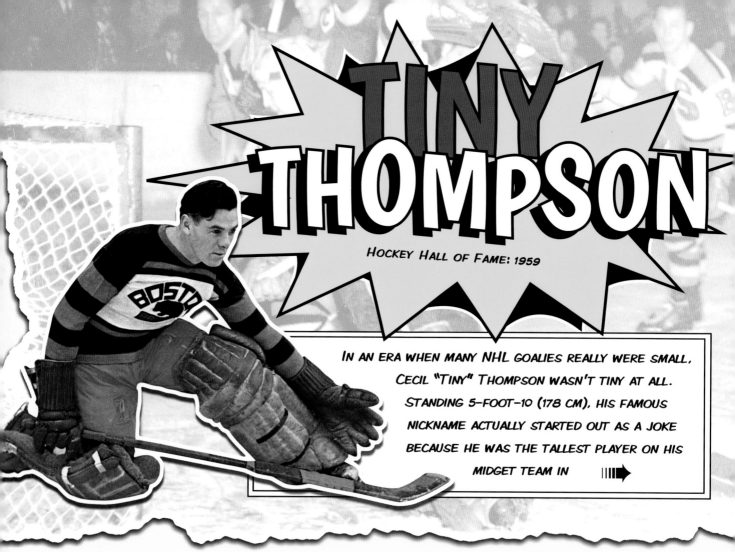

TINY THOMPSON

HOCKEY HALL OF FAME: 1959

IN AN ERA WHEN MANY NHL GOALIES REALLY WERE SMALL, CECIL "TINY" THOMPSON WASN'T TINY AT ALL. STANDING 5-FOOT-10 (178 CM), HIS FAMOUS NICKNAME ACTUALLY STARTED OUT AS A JOKE BECAUSE HE WAS THE TALLEST PLAYER ON HIS MIDGET TEAM IN

Parallel Puckstopper

ROY WORTERS (HHOF: 1969)

There was no joking when it came to Roy Worters' nickname. Standing 5-foot-3 (160 cm) and weighing only 135 pounds (61 kg), Worters was known as "Shrimp." He may have been small, but he was a big talent! Worters played on bad teams his whole career, but did his best to keep them competitive. In 1928–29, he became the first goalie in NHL history to win the Hart Trophy as league MVP! Only two teams scored fewer goals than his New York Americans that year, but Worters' 13 shutouts and 1.15 goals-against average got them into the playoffs.

Calgary, Alberta. And once he got to the NHL, the term "Tiny" best described his goals-against average!

Thompson began his NHL career with the Boston Bruins in 1928–29. In his first game, he earned a shutout in a 1–0 win over the Pittsburgh Pirates. Thompson went on to post 12 shutouts that season and had a goals-against average of 1.15. That season was the lowest-scoring season in NHL history, and Thompson's average ranked second in the league behind George Hainsworth. In the playoffs, Thompson out-dueled Hainsworth with two more shutouts when Boston swept Montreal in the semifinals. The Bruins then swept the New York Rangers to win the Stanley Cup for the first time!

The next season, 1929–30, the NHL introduced new passing rules that led to more scoring. Still, Thompson's 2.19 goals-against average was the best in the league, and he won the Vezina Trophy for the first time. He led the NHL in wins as well, as Boston had an amazing record of 38–5–1 during the 44-game regular season. That year, however, Hainsworth and the Canadiens got their revenge in the playoffs when Montreal upset Boston to win the Stanley Cup.

Thompson was a four-time All Star and he won the Vezina Trophy four times in his career, which was a league record when he retired from the NHL in 1940.

Did You Know?

PAUL THOMPSON OF THE RANGERS BECAME THE FIRST NHL PLAYER TO SCORE AGAINST HIS OWN BROTHER WHEN HE BEAT TINY THOMPSON ON MARCH 18, 1930.

ROBERTO LUONGO, LIKE Tiny Thompson, earned his puck-stopping reputation early in his career. Unlike Thompson, though, Loungo built his reputation playing on bad teams. In his first NHL game he stopped 43 shots for the New York Islanders. He later spent time playing with the Florida Panthers where he regularly faced the most shots in the league. Luongo played eight seasons with the Vancouver Canucks, leading them all the way to Game 7 of the 2010 Stanley Cup final. He also backstopped Canada to a gold medal at the 2010 Olympics. Luongo is now stopping pucks in Florida again.

MODERN MATCH
ROBERTO LUONGO

TONY ESPOSITO

HOCKEY HALL OF FAME: 1988

WHILE HIS OLDER BROTHER PHIL WAS SMASHING NHL SCORING RECORDS, TONY ESPOSITO MADE A NAME FOR HIMSELF AS ONE OF THE GREATEST GOALIES IN HOCKEY HISTORY. TONY TOOK A LONG TIME TO ARRIVE IN THE NHL. HE WAS 26 YEARS OLD BY THE TIME HE PLAYED ▭▭▶

Blast FROM THE Past

GEORGE HAINSWORTH (HHOF: 1961)

George Hainsworth wasn't flashy. He didn't make diving saves or shout at other players. He just stopped the puck better than anyone else. In 1928–29, Hainsworth recorded an amazing 22 shutouts during the 44-game regular season. His performance earned him the Vezina Trophy for the third year in a row! Hainsworth never had another season like 1928–29 — nobody ever has! — but he did help Montreal win the Stanley Cup in 1930 and 1931. He later played three seasons with the Toronto Maple Leafs and led the league in wins twice. His 94 career shutouts rank him third all-time in NHL history.

his first full season in 1969–70. Today, that would make him too old to win the Calder Trophy as rookie of the year, but back then it would have been crazy to give the award to anybody else.

Though he came from Sault Ste. Marie, Ontario, Esposito was one of the first big stars to make it to the NHL from an American college. After three stellar seasons at Michigan Tech University, he signed with the Montreal Canadiens in 1967. Esposito saw a bit of action with the team in 1968–69, and even got his name engraved on the Stanley Cup when the Canadiens won it that year. But Montreal had a lot of great goalies. They didn't hang on to Esposito, and the Chicago Black Hawks picked him up. Goalies almost always wore No. 1 or No. 30 in those days, but Esposito wanted something to make himself stand out so he asked to wear No. 35. However,

Did You Know?

TONY ESPOSITO SHARED THE NET WITH KEN DRYDEN ON TEAM CANADA DURING THE 1972 SUMMIT SERIES AGAINST THE SOVIET UNION.

the numbers that really stood out during the 1969–70 season were the spectacular statistics he had. Esposito led the NHL with 15 shutouts that season. Nobody had posted that many in more than 40 years, and nobody has done so since. Esposito won both the Vezina and the Calder Trophies that season. He later won the Vezina Trophy two more times.

Playing with his legs spread wide and relying on a lightning-fast glove hand, Esposito went on to become the fourth goalie in NHL history to record 400 career wins.

George Hainsworth

1928–29:
The Year of the Shutout

The 1928–29 season was the lowest-scoring season in NHL history. The two teams playing on any given night combined to score an average of less than 3 goals per game. In addition to George Hainsworth's 22 shutouts, seven other goalies had 10 or more shutouts that season. Hainsworth led the league with a 0.92 goals-against average, but the starting goalies on the other nine teams in the league all had averages ranging from 1.15 to 1.85. At one point during the season, the Chicago Black Hawks went eight straight games without scoring a single goal!

VLADISLAV TRETIAK

Vladislav Tretiak wasn't supposed to be that good. In 1972 his Soviet (Russian) National Team played against the top stars from the NHL in an eight-game tournament called the Summit Series. The Russian team had dominated international hockey since the 1960s but had never played against NHL players. ||||➡

FROM THE VAULT

WORLD CLASS JERSEY

In league play in Russia, Vladislav Tretiak helped the Red Army win 13 championships in 14 seasons from 1970 to 1984. He was a First-Team All-Star every season! Internationally, Tretiak played at the World Championships 13 times and won 10 World titles! He also played at the Olympics four times, winning three gold medals and one silver. In all, he played 98 international games and posted a goals-against average of 1.78. Tretiak wore this jersey at the 1973 World Championship in Moscow. The Russians were a perfect 10-and-0 that year and won the World title.

They were expected to lose badly against the mighty Canadians. Instead, Canada narrowly escaped defeat.

Before the series, Team Canada sent scouts to watch the Russians. The game they saw Tretiak play was on the night before he got married. He didn't stop many shots. "I couldn't concentrate on the game," he later admitted. The scouts reported that Tretiak was the weakest Russian player. But in reality, Tretiak was one of the best goalies in the world. His stellar play in the Summit Series made him incredibly popular, even in Canada. Back then, Russians weren't allowed to leave their country to play in the NHL, but the Montreal Canadiens tried for years without success to bring him over.

Tretiak was only 15 years old when he began practicing with Moscow's Central Red Army, the top team in Russia. Two years later,

in 1969–70, he became the team's starting goalie. Tretiak made his first appearance at the World Championships in 1970 and at the Olympics in 1972. He starred with the Central Red Army and the national team until 1984. The Russians were nearly unbeatable in those years, and they played many exhibition games against NHL teams too. On New Year's Eve in 1975, Tretiak led the Red Army to a 3–3 tie with the Montreal Canadiens despite being outshot 38–13. Many people consider this to be the greatest game ever played.

MODERN MATCH
HENRIK LUNDQVIST

VLADISLAV TRETIAK NEVER played in the NHL, but many other great goalies from Europe certainly have. Two of the best over the years were Dominik Hasek of the Czech Republic and Miikka Kiprusoff of Finland. Today, there are top goalies in the NHL from many different countries, including Sweden's Henrik Lundqvist. Lundqvist joined the New York Rangers in 2005–06 and was so good that people began calling him "King Henrik." Lundqvist was the first goalie in NHL history to win 30 games or more in each of his first seven seasons. He won the Vezina Trophy in 2011–12.

ED BELFOUR

HOCKEY HALL OF FAME: 2011

NO ONE IN THE NHL WANTED ED BELFOUR AFTER HIS JUNIOR HOCKEY CAREER. HE WASN'T DRAFTED INTO THE NHL, BUT THAT DIDN'T STOP HIM FROM TRYING TO MAKE THE PROS. FINALLY, AFTER LEADING THE UNIVERSITY OF NORTH DAKOTA TO THE NCAA ▐▐▐▶

Parallel Puckstopper

TOM BARRASSO

A few years before Ed Belfour won both the Calder Trophy and the Vezina Trophy, Tom Barrasso did the same thing when he broke into the NHL with the Buffalo Sabres in 1983–84. Amazingly, Barrasso was just 18 years old that season and joined the NHL directly from high school! Barrasso was traded to Pittsburgh early in the 1988–89 season and helped the Penguins win the Stanley Cup in 1991. They won it again in 1992, beating Belfour and the Blackhawks that year. Barrasso is a member of the United States Hockey Hall of Fame.

championship in 1986–87, he signed with the Chicago Blackhawks.

In 1990, the Blackhawks hired Russian goalie legend Vladislav Tretiak to coach their goalies. Belfour worked with Tretiak at training camp and won the job as Chicago's starting goalie. He went on to have one of the greatest seasons any rookie goalie has ever had. Belfour played 74 out of 80 possible games and set a club record that still stands with 43 wins! He led Chicago to the best record in the NHL and also led the league with a 2.47 goals-against average. Not only did Belfour win the Calder Trophy as the NHL's best rookie, but also the Vezina Trophy as the league's best goalie. His win marked only the fourth time a goalie had won both awards in the same season. Belfour led Chicago to the Stanley Cup final the following year, and won the Vezina Trophy again in 1992–93.

Belfour was a hard worker who expected nothing but the best effort, every night, from himself and his teammates. Sometimes, that demanding attitude made him hard to get along with. Chicago traded Belfour to San Jose in 1997 and the next season he signed with the Dallas Stars. Belfour posted a career-best 1.88 goals-against average with the Stars in 1997–98 and won the Stanley Cup with them in 1999. He ended his career with the Florida Panthers in 2006–07. His 484 wins rank him third all-time in NHL history.

Did You Know?

AFTER LEAVING CHICAGO, ED BELFOUR WORE NO. 20 IN HONOR OF HIS FORMER GOALIE COACH AND HALL OF FAMER, VLADISLAV TRETIAK, WHO'D WORN NO. 20 DURING HIS CAREER.

UNDRAFTED HALL of FAMERS

For most future NHL stars, their career begins with the excitement of hearing their name called at the NHL Draft. The NHL held its first draft in 1963, and since then, nearly every player who has been inducted to the Hockey Hall of Fame has been drafted … but not all of them! Ed Belfour is the only undrafted goalie currently in the Hall of Fame. Borje Salming and Peter Statsny were never drafted either, but signed as free agents from Europe. American Joe Mullen and Canadians Dino Ciccarelli and Adam Oates are the only other undrafted Hall of Famers.

HOCKEY HALL OF FAME: 2000

Joe MULLEN

TURK BRODA

HOCKEY HALL OF FAME: 1967

TURK BRODA WAS THE FIRST GOALIE IN NHL HISTORY TO WIN 300 GAMES. THOUGH HIS CAREER ENDED MORE THAN 60 YEARS AGO, HIS 302 VICTORIES ARE STILL THE MOST IN THE HISTORY OF THE TORONTO MAPLE LEAFS. IN FACT, JOHNNY BOWER HAS THE SECOND-MOST WINS OF ANY OTHER MAPLE LEAFS' ‖‖➡

RILEY HERN (HHOF: 1962)

Blast FROM THE Past

Like Turk Broda, Riley Hern had a reputation for winning championships. Hern played in the early 1900s when hockey players first got paid to play the game. Pittsburgh was the center of pro hockey in those days, and Hern helped the Pittsburgh Keystones win the American championship in 1901–02. He later won two more U.S. titles with another team. When Canadian teams began to pay their players in 1906–07, Hern returned to his home country. He joined the Montreal Wanderers and helped them win the Stanley Cup in 1907, 1908 and 1910!

goalie, and he is still 83 behind Broda! Good as he was during the regular season, Broda was even better in the playoffs. He led the Maple Leafs to five Stanley Cup championships and boasted a goals-against average of 1.98 in 101 career playoff games.

Broda's real first name was Walter. The most common story about how he got the nickname "Turk" is that the large freckles he had when he was a boy looked like the spots on a turkey egg. Broda grew up in Brandon, Manitoba and attracted the attention of scouts from Detroit while playing in Brandon and Winnipeg in the early 1930s. In 1936, the Maple Leafs bought Broda from the Red Wings for almost $8,000! That may not seem like much money today, but it was a huge price to pay for a minor-league goalie during The Great Depression.

Many people thought the Leafs had been

Did You Know?

IN 1941–42, TURK BRODA BECAME THE FIRST TORONTO GOALIE TO WIN THE VEZINA TROPHY. HE WON IT AGAIN IN 1947–48.

cheated, but Broda soon won over the fans in Toronto with his outgoing personality. His hard work in practice impressed his teammates. After the team reached the finals in 1938, 1939 and 1940, Broda and the Maple Leafs won the Stanley Cup in 1942. He later spent two years with the Canadian Army in World War II, and when he returned to Toronto he led the Maple Leafs to the most successful time in team history. They won the Stanley Cup three years in a row from 1947 to 1949, and then won it again in 1951.

TOO BIG TO FAIL:
Broda's Battle of the Bulge

Turk Broda didn't really look like an athlete, but despite his chubby appearance he was a hard worker. Even so, when Toronto struggled early in the 1949–50 season, Maple Leafs owner Conn Smythe ordered Broda out of the lineup until he lost some weight. Newspapers loved the story of Broda's "Battle of the Bulge." They showed pictures of him sitting on a scale while eating a steak or drinking juice for dinner while trying to lose weight. Broda was back after a week of dieting and went on to post nine shutouts that season, which was a career high.

GERRY CHEEVERS

HOCKEY HALL OF FAME: 1985

GERRY CHEEVERS WAS A GOALIE WHO DIDN'T LIKE TO PRACTICE. HE STARTED PLAYING HOCKEY WHEN GOALIES DIDN'T WEAR MASKS, AND IN THOSE DAYS GOALIE EQUIPMENT WAS OKAY TO STOP PUCKS, BUT IT DIDN'T STOP MANY BRUISES. SO CHEEVERS HATED PRACTICE BECAUSE HE NEVER FELT IT WAS ||||▶

FROM THE VAULT

PAINTED MASKS

Former NHL goalie Brian Hayward wore this mask while playing with the San Jose Sharks in 1992–93. The first goalie to feature a design on his mask was Gerry Cheevers. Cheevers was faking an injury to get out of practice after taking a soft shot in the face. As a joke, he had the trainer paint a line of stitches onto his white, fiberglass mask. It got a big laugh, so every time Cheevers got hit in the face, he added more stitches. Over the years, the black stitch-marks on Cheevers' mask became his trademark.

worth the risk of getting hurt. When Cheevers was young he also liked to roam from his net to play the puck. His coach with the St. Michael's Majors hated this. To try and teach Cheevers a lesson, the coach made him play a handful of games as a left winger during the 1960–61 season. "I was never so happy to get back in goal!" Cheevers said afterward.

Cheevers was slated behind Johnny Bower and Terry Sawchuk on the Toronto Maple Leafs roster and only played briefly with the Leafs before he was picked up by Boston in 1965. Cheevers shared the Bruins' net with veteran Eddie Johnson, who helped him adjust to life in the NHL. Soon, Cheevers took over as the team's number-one goalie. The Bruins were the worst team in the league at the time, but the addition of Bobby Orr, Phil Esposito and others turned them around in a hurry! Cheevers still didn't like to practice, but he earned a reputation as a goalie who played his best when it mattered most, helping Boston win the Stanley Cup in 1970 and 1972. During the 1971–72 season, Cheevers set a record that still stands by playing 32 games in a row without a loss. He had 24 wins and eight ties during his streak.

Cheevers helped the Bruins reach the Stanley Cup finals again in 1977 and 1978. He retired after the 1979–80 season and spent the next four-and-a-half seasons as Boston's coach.

Did You Know?

GERRY CHEEVERS WAS ONE OF THE FIRST NHL SUPERSTARS TO LEAVE THE LEAGUE AND JOIN THE RIVAL WORLD HOCKEY ASSOCIATION IN 1972–73.

MODERN MATCH
TUUKKA RASK

AFTER A STELLAR junior career in his native Finland, Tuukka Rask began his NHL career as property of the Toronto Maple Leafs before joining the Bruins, just like Gerry Cheevers. Toronto took Rask in the first round of the 2005 NHL Draft, but traded him to Boston one year later. After spending one more year in Finland, Rask joined the Bruins for the 2007–08 season and got his first NHL win against the Maple Leafs! Rask led the NHL in goals-against average during the 2009–10 season and has been one of the league's best goalies ever since.

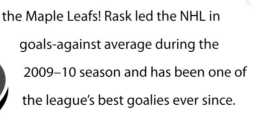

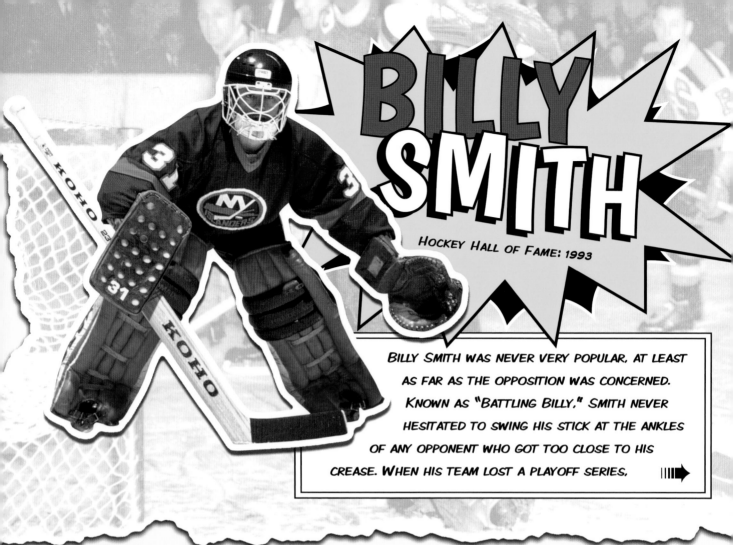

BILLY SMITH

HOCKEY HALL OF FAME: 1993

BILLY SMITH WAS NEVER VERY POPULAR, AT LEAST AS FAR AS THE OPPOSITION WAS CONCERNED. KNOWN AS "BATTLING BILLY," SMITH NEVER HESITATED TO SWING HIS STICK AT THE ANKLES OF ANY OPPONENT WHO GOT TOO CLOSE TO HIS CREASE. WHEN HIS TEAM LOST A PLAYOFF SERIES, ▐▐▐▶

Parallel Puckstopper

RON HEXTALL

On November 28, 1979, Billy Smith became the first goalie in NHL history to be credited with scoring a goal. In reality, Smith was simply the last Islander to touch the puck before a Colorado Rockies player accidentally shot it into his own open net. The first goalie to actually shoot the puck the length of the ice and score into an open net was Ron Hextall of the Philadelphia Flyers on December 8, 1987. Like Smith, Hextall was an aggressive goalie who often swung his stick at opponents and sometimes got into fights with other goalies.

Smith often skipped the ritual of shaking hands with the other team. He would yell at referees and even at his own teammates (sometimes), but that was usually just to fire them up. Mostly, though, Billy Smith battled to stop the puck, and he was pretty good when it came to that!

The Los Angeles Kings originally selected Smith in the 1970 NHL Draft. After spending most of the next two years in the minors, he was picked up by the New York Islanders. Smith struggled with his new team for the first two seasons, but the Islanders quickly became a contender. Smith emerged as the Islanders' number-one goalie in 1974–75, but he usually shared the playing time — first with Glenn "Chico" Resch and later with Rollie Melanson and Kelly Hrudy. However, when the playoffs rolled around, it was Smith the Islanders counted on.

By the end of the 1970s, the Islanders had developed a reputation as a top team in the regular season that always seemed to struggle in the playoffs. That all changed in the spring of 1980. That year, Smith played in 20 of the Islanders' 21 playoff games and helped them win the Stanley Cup. It was the first of four straight championship seasons for Smith and the Islanders. During those years, Smith played 72 playoff games and posted a record of 57–13! He won the Conn Smythe Trophy as playoff MVP during the team's final Stanley Cup run in 1983.

Did You Know?

BILLY SMITH WAS THE FIRST GOALIE TO WIN THE VEZINA TROPHY WHEN NHL GENERAL MANAGERS BEGAN TO VOTE FOR THE AWARD IN 1981-82.

DOUBLE THE FUN:
The Two-Goalie System

Before the 1965–66 season, NHL teams only had to dress one goalie for every game. Some teams began using a backup goalie as early as the 1920s, but it was pretty common for teams to use the same goalie all season long. Even when teams did use a backup, it was usually because their regular starter had suffered a serious injury. However, from the mid 1960s until the end of the 1980s, the "two-goalie system" became very popular. Like Billy Smith's New York Islanders, most teams had two, or even three, goalies they rotated throughout the season.

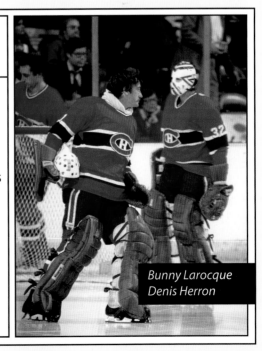

Bunny Larocque
Denis Herron

GRANT FUHR

HOCKEY HALL OF FAME: 2003

WHEN GRANT FUHR ARRIVED IN THE NHL WITH THE EDMONTON OILERS IN 1981-82, GOAL SCORING WAS AT AN ALL-TIME HIGH. FUHR'S TEAMMATE WAYNE GRETZKY NOTCHED A RECORD 92 GOALS THAT SEASON AND LED THE NHL WITH 212 POINTS! FUHR WAS JUST 19 YEARS OLD, BUT ▐▐▐▶

SCORING TODAY IS nothing like it was when Wayne Gretzky starred for Edmonton. Still, playing on a Pittsburgh team that features Sidney Crosby, Evgeni Malkin, James Neal and Chris Kunitz, people often compare Marc-Andre Fleury to Grant Fuhr. Pittsburgh made Fleury the first pick in the 2003 NHL Draft, which is rare for a goalie. Like Fuhr, Fleury made his first NHL start as a 19-year-old and was soon ranked among the top goalies in the NHL. During game seven of the Stanley Cup final in 2009, Fleury made a spectacular diving save with two seconds left to preserve Pittsburgh's victory.

MODERN MATCH
MARC-ANDRE FLEURY

he won 28 games and lost only five. He became the youngest goalie in NHL history to play in the All-Star Game and finished third in voting for rookie of the year. He was second behind Billy Smith in voting for the Vezina Trophy.

Playing with the high-scoring Oilers, Fuhr didn't always get a lot of help from his defense. His goals-against average was usually high, but he gained a reputation as someone who rarely let the other team score the big goal. Fuhr might give up four in a game, but only if Edmonton scored five or more. If the game was close, opponents found it almost impossible to beat Fuhr for the goal they needed to tie it up or go ahead. Edmonton's all-out attack helped Fuhr set an NHL record for goalies with 14 assists in 1983–84 while his goaltending helped the Oilers win the Stanley Cup that season. They

won it again three times over the next four years!

Fuhr won the Vezina Trophy in 1987–88 but his play slipped the following season and he later admitted to using drugs. Fuhr worked hard to recover and he played backup for Edmonton when they won the Stanley Cup in 1989–90. He was traded in 1991, and played for five teams over the next nine years, always putting up solid numbers. Though injuries finally slowed him down in his final season of 1999–2000, Fuhr became just the sixth goalie in NHL history to top 400 wins!

Parallel Puckstopper

ANDY MOOG

Andy Moog joined the Oilers in 1980–81 and led them to a stunning playoff upset of Montreal that spring. From 1982–83 through 1986–87, Moog shared netminding duties in Edmonton with Grant Fuhr. But, when it came time for the playoffs, Moog spent most of his time on the bench. He was traded to Boston in 1988 and later played for Dallas and Montreal before retiring in 1998. Though Moog was overshadowed by bigger names throughout his career, his regular-season record of 372–209–88 ranks him among the most successful goalies in NHL history!

FRANK BRIMSEK

HOCKEY HALL OF FAME: 1966

A FEW DAYS BEFORE THE 1938–39 SEASON, BRUINS GOALIE TINY THOMPSON SUFFERED A BAD CUT ABOVE HIS RIGHT EYE. FRANK BRIMSEK WAS CALLED UP FROM THE MINORS AND OPENED THE SEASON WITH TWO STRAIGHT WINS. THOMPSON RETURNED TO THE NET AFTER THAT, BUT BRUINS BOSS ART ROSS LIKED WHAT HE'D SEEN OF THE NEW YOUNG ROOKIE. ▐▐▐▶

Blast FROM THE Past

ALEX CONNELL (HHOF: 1958)

The same way Frank Brimsek replaced Boston legend Tiny Thompson in goal, Alex Connell replaced Ottawa legend Clint Benedict in 1924–25. Connell recorded seven shutouts that season to lead the NHL for the first of five times in his career. He led Ottawa to the Stanley Cup in 1926–27, and posted a league-best 15 shutouts in 1927–28, including a streak of six in a row to set a record that has never been beaten! Connell finished his career with the Montreal Maroons. There he led the NHL in shutouts one last time with nine in 1934–35.

A few weeks later, he traded Thompson to Detroit and made Brimsek his goaltender. Boston fans, and even some of the players, weren't sure about the move. There was some grumbling when Brimsek lost his first game, but he bounced back with three straight shutouts. After a 3–2 win in his next game, Brimsek recorded three more shutouts. In his first eight games as an NHL regular, Brimsek had seven wins and six shutouts! He'd be known as "Mr. Zero" from then on.

Brimsek finished the 1938–39 season with a record of 33–9–1, leading the league with his 33 wins, 10 shutouts and 1.56 goals-against average. Brimsek became the first goalie in NHL history to win the Vezina Trophy as best goalie and the Calder Trophy as rookie of the year in the same season. He also led the Bruins to the Stanley Cup. Brimsek would never have another season quite as amazing as his first, but he still had plenty of success. Brimsek and the Bruins won the Stanley Cup again in 1940–41 and he won a second Vezina Trophy in 1941–42.

Over his first eight seasons in the NHL, Brimsek was named either a First-Team or Second-Team All-Star every year. Making the streak even more incredible is the fact that after his first five years, Brimsek missed the next two seasons while serving with the United States Navy during World War II. He then had three more All-Star seasons.

Did You Know?

FRANK BRIMSEK BECAME AN ORIGINAL MEMBER OF THE UNITED STATES HOCKEY HALL OF FAME WHEN IT OPENED IN HIS HOMETOWN OF EVELETH, MINNESOTA, IN 1973.

MODERN MATCH
JONATHAN QUICK

IT WAS RARE to find an American-born player in the league when Frank Brimsek played in the NHL. Today, Jonathan Quick is one of about a dozen American goalies playing in the league. He became the number-one goalie for the Los Angeles Kings in 2008–09. During the 2011–12 season, Quick led the NHL with 10 shutouts and was second with a 1.95 goals-against average. When the Kings won the Stanley Cup that year, he was named the most valuable player of the playoffs. Quick has represented the United States at the Olympics in 2010 and 2014.

EDDIE GIACOMIN

HOCKEY HALL OF FAME: 1987

WHEN HE WAS 15 YEARS OLD, EDDIE GIACOMIN ATTENDED A JUNIOR TRYOUT FOR THE DETROIT RED WINGS. A SCOUT SENT HIM BACK HOME TO SUDBURY, ONTARIO, TELLING HIM HE WASN'T GOOD ENOUGH. "HE SAID I'D NEVER MAKE IT," GIACOMIN REMEMBERED. "HE SAID I SHOULD FORGET ABOUT BEING A GOALIE." GIACOMIN DIDN'T FORGET. HE WORKED HARD AND GOT ▌▌▶

LESTER PATRICK — Blast FROM THE Past

HOCKEY HALL OF FAME: 1947

Lester Patrick was a big name in hockey, but he wasn't really a goalie. As a star player from 1903 to 1926, he mostly played defense. From 1926 until 1947, he was the coach and general manager of the New York Rangers. A few times during his playing career, Patrick made emergency appearances in goal. Still, it was a shock when the 44-year-old coach took over in the Rangers net midway through Game 2 of the 1928 Stanley Cup final. The team's regular goalie had been injured, and Patrick led the Rangers to a 2–1 victory in overtime!

a little help from his older brother, Rollie. A minor-league team in Washington wanted Eddie's older brother to come and play the last few games of the 1958–59 season, but Rollie didn't want to go. He sent Eddie instead, and it was the start of six full seasons that the younger Giacomin played in the minor leagues. Finally, Eddie got his chance in the NHL with the New York Rangers in 1965–66. The Rangers weren't a very good team. They missed the playoffs that year for the seventh time in eight seasons, but Giacomin was sharp and

Did You Know?

THE RANGERS RETIRED EDDIE GIACOMIN'S NO. 1 IN 1989, MAKING HIM JUST THE SECOND PLAYER IN TEAM HISTORY TO HAVE HIS NUMBER RETIRED.

he took over the number-one job in the Rangers' goal the next year. He was the busiest goalie in the NHL in 1966–67, playing 68 games during the 70-game season and leading the NHL with 30 wins and nine shutouts. The Rangers made the playoffs, and Giacomin was selected as a First-Team All-Star! During the eight full seasons he spent as the starting goalie in New York, the Rangers never missed the playoffs and Giacomin helped them reach the Stanley Cup finals in 1972.

Like Jacques Plante, Giacomin made acrobatic saves and liked to roam from the crease to play the puck. Unlike Plante, he didn't like wearing a mask because he thought he saw the puck better without one. Giacomin only started wearing a mask in 1970. He had a great season in 1970–71, sharing the Vezina Trophy with his backup goalie Gilles Villemure.

RANGER LEGENDS

Eddie Giacomin never won a Stanley Cup. In fact, the Rangers went without a Stanley Cup win for 54 years from 1940 to 1994! Goalie Mike Richter was one of the Rangers' heroes in 1993–94. After having shared the net with John Vanbiesbrouck since joining the team in 1989, Richter was handed the number-one job in 1993–94. He set a franchise record with 42 wins and was also the winning goalie in all 16 playoff victories the Rangers posted as they won the Stanley Cup! Richter was the first goalie to win 300 games with the Rangers. His No. 35 was retired in 2004.

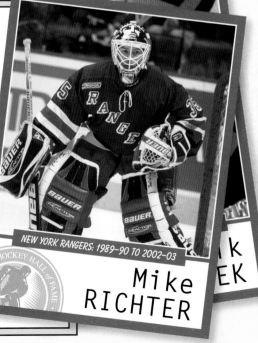

NEW YORK RANGERS: 1989–90 TO 2002–03

Mike RICHTER

CHARLIE GARDINER

HOCKEY HALL OF FAME: 1945

WHEN CHARLIE GARDINER PLAYED HE WAS OFTEN THE BEST PLAYER ON HIS TEAM — AND EVEN THE BEST PLAYER ON EITHER TEAM! IF HIS CAREER HADN'T BEEN CUT TRAGICALLY SHORT AFTER JUST SEVEN SEASONS, IT'S POSSIBLE GARDINER MAY HAVE BECOME THE GREATEST GOALIE OF ALL TIME.

GARDINER WAS BORN IN EDINBURGH, ▌▌▌▶

IT TOOK COREY Crawford awhile to establish himself in Chicago. The Blackhawks chose him in the second round of the 2003 NHL Draft, but he only played in a handful of games until the 2010–11 season. He became the team's number-one goalie that year and was named to the NHL's All-Rookie Team. Crawford struggled the following season, but bounced back strong in 2012–13. He and Ray Emery combined to help Chicago win the Jennings Trophy for allowing the fewest goals. In the playoffs, Crawford was the main man in net as Chicago won the Stanley Cup!

MODERN MATCH
COREY CRAWFORD

Scotland, but came to Canada at the age of seven and grew up in Winnipeg. Often known as "Chuck" instead of Charlie, he rose through the hockey ranks in his new hometown. When he was 21, Gardiner turned pro with the minor-league Winnipeg Maroons. Two years later, in 1927–28, he was on the NHL's Chicago Black Hawks. The Black Hawks were only in their second season, and they were bad. Gardiner always had to make plenty of big saves to keep his team in the game, and while Chicago usually lost, Gardiner was often praised for his fine play. People also liked his positive attitude. He was often heard shouting encouragement to teammates or joking with fans. After two dreadful seasons, Gardiner led Chicago to the playoffs in 1929–30. In 1930–31, the Black Hawks reached the Stanley Cup final, but lost to Montreal. Still, the best — and

the worst — was yet to come.

Gardiner won the Vezina Trophy in 1931–32 and won it again in 1933–34. That year, he led Chicago to the finals once again. This time they beat Detroit to win the Stanley Cup with Gardiner earning a shutout in overtime in the last game. Unfortunately, Gardiner had played much of that season with a badly infected tonsil in his throat. He ignored the pain, but the infection spread throughout his body. Back home in Winnipeg after the season, Gardiner collapsed and was rushed to the hospital. He died on June 13, 1934 at the age of 29.

Blast FROM THE Past BOUSE HUTTON (HHOF: 1962)

Like Charlie Gardiner, Bouse Hutton had a short career but the reasons for it were very different. Hutton played hockey at a time in Canada when players had to be amateurs — they weren't allowed to be paid to play sports. When Hutton accepted money to play lacrosse in 1904, he had to give up his hockey career. Hutton played in his hometown of Ottawa from 1899 to 1904 and helped the "Silver Seven" win the Stanley Cup in 1903 and 1904. He also won national championships with Ottawa teams in lacrosse and football.

INDEX

PHOTO CREDITS

T=Top, B= Bottom

All illustrations © George Todorovic

Hockey Hall of Fame

Graphic Artists/HHOF 18T, 20B, 22T, 28T; Steve Babineau/HHOF 15B; Bereswill/HHOF 5 (Fuhr), 38T; Howie Borrow/HHOF 19B; Hockey Hall of Fame 12T, 24T, 27B, 42B; Doug MacLellan/HHOF 5 (Roy), 10T, 12B, 30B, 31B, 39B; Matthew Manor/HHOF 6B, 10B, 16B, 34B; Mecca/HHOF 26T; O-Pee-Chee/HHOF 18B, 34T, 36B, 37B; Portnoy/HHOF 36T; Frank Prazak/HHOF 42T; Chris Relke/HHOF 30T; James Rice/HHOF 14T; Hal Roth/HHOF 28B; Dave Sandford/HHOF 43B; Thompson/HHOF 9B; Imperial Oil–Turofsky/HHOF 5 (Bower, Hall, Plante), 6T, 8T, 8B, 16T, 20T, 23B, 32T, 33B, 40T, 44T.

All images used for the cover are listed above as they appear in the book.

Icon Sports Images

Justin Berl/Icon SMI 29B, 38B; Jerome Davis/Icon SMI 5 (Price), 22B; Rich Graessle/Icon SMI 7B; Fred Kfoury/Icon SMI 5 (Rask), 35B; Gary Rothstein/Icon SMI 25B; Ric Tapia/Icon SMI 41B; Warren Wimmer/Icon SMI 5 (Crawford), 44B.